Picture credits:
l: Left, r: Right, t: Top, b: Bottom, c: Centre

Front Cover: Background: Adrian Chesterman/ Istockphoto,
tr: Sebastian Kaulitzki/ Shutterstock, mr: Adrian Chesterman/ Istockphoto,
bl: David Coder/ Istockphoto, br: Miles Kelly/ Fotolibra.

Backcover: Background: Adrian Chesterman/ Istockphoto,
tl: Ritu Manoj Jethani/ Shutterstock, tm: Alexal/ Shutterstock

Border Images : Ritu Manoj Jethani/ Shutterstock, Ismael Montero Verdu/ Shutterstock.

Inside :
7b: Adrian Chesterman/ Istockphoto, 12t: David Coder/ Istockphoto, 12b: Photo Researchers, Inc./ Photolibrary,
13: John Kirinic/ Shutterstock, 14t: Csaba Fikker/ Istockphoto, 14b: Ritu Manoj Jethani/ Shutterstock,
16b: Ty Smith/ Istockphoto, 17b: July Flower/ Shutterstock, 20-21m: Miles Kelly/ Fotolibra,
22-23t: Christian Darkin / Shutterstock, 24b: Ralf Juergen Kraft/ Shutterstock, 27b: Jozef Sedmak/ Shutterstock,
34: Sebastian Kaulitzki/ Shutterstock, 35t: Julien Grondin/ Shutterstock, 35b: John Kirinic/ Shutterstock,
36: Frederick R. Matzen/ Shutterstock, 37t: Ismael Montero Verdu/ Shutterstock, 37mr: Alexal/ Shutterstock,
37bl: Terry Walsh/ Shutterstock, 38t: Jim Jurica/ Istockphoto, 38b: Dawn Hagan/ Istockphoto,
39: Tammy Bryngelson/ Istockphoto, 40: Ismael Montero Verdu/ Shutterstock, 41: Elena Ray/ Shutterstock.

Copyright: North Parade Publishing Ltd.,
4 North Parade, Bath, BA1 1LF, UK

Discover the Prehistoric World of

DINOSAURS
CONTENTS

Evolution Through Time

It is generally thought that earth was created by a 'big bang', about 4,600 million years ago. The history of earth is divided into lengths of time or eras. Each era is further divided into smaller time spans known as periods.

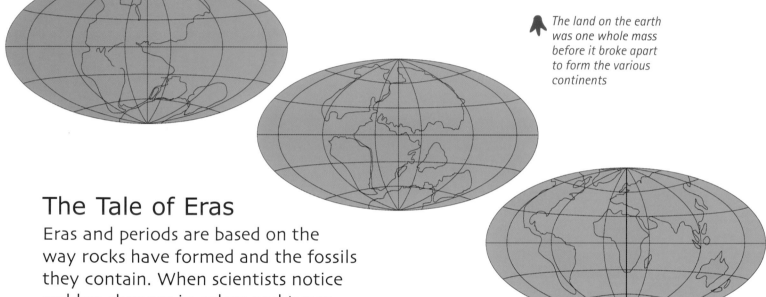

The land on the earth was one whole mass before it broke apart to form the various continents

The Tale of Eras

Eras and periods are based on the way rocks have formed and the fossils they contain. When scientists notice sudden changes in colors and types of rocks they mark these changes as the beginning of new eras or periods. The history of earth has been divided into four eras: the Precambrian period is the birth of earth up to the Cambrian explosion, when many forms of life developed; this is when the Paleozoic Era started. During this time organisms large enough to be seen by the naked eye evolved; the middle period, or Mesozoic Era, is the era of reptiles, including the dinosaurs; the extinction of dinosaurs marked the end of this era and the beginning of recent life, or the Cenozoic Era. This era saw the rise of mammals including humans.

The Mesozoic Era: about 245-65 million years ago

The Mesozoic Era spanned about 200 million years. During this time earth was very different to how it is now. The climate was warmer, the seasons were very mild and there was no Polar ice. The continents were joined together at the beginning of the Mesozoic Era and started breaking apart toward the middle of the Mesozoic Era. During this time, sea reptiles, dinosaurs, mammals, birds and flowering plants came into being. The Mesozoic Era is divided into three periods: Triassic, Jurassic and Cretaceous.

Triassic Period: about 245-208 million years ago

The earliest period of the Mesozoic Era is known as the Triassic period. It was during this period that small dinosaurs, such as Coelophysis, Euparkeria and Staurikosaurus, trod the earth.

Dino Facts

Originally the continents were joined together, forming one super continent known as Pangaea. The Jurassic period saw the division of Pangaea into Laurasia and Gondwana, which, in turn, facilitated the evolution of various species of dinosaurs.

Many kinds of dinosaurs roamed the earth during the Mesozoic Era

Jurassic Period: about 208-146 million years ago

This was the period when dinosaurs began to flourish. As the continents began to break up, climate began to change. This in turn enabled the growth of many kinds of plants and the development of varied animals. Dinosaurs were the dominant land animals. Diplodocus, Brachiosaurus, Apatosaurus, Allosaurus and Stegosaurus were abundant in this period.

Cretaceous Period: about 146-65 million years ago

Dinosaurs thrived during this period. Tyrannosaurus rex, Giganotosaurus, Triceratops, Parasaurolophus, and Anatotitan are among the famous dinosaurs of this time. The era also saw the extinction of dinosaurs.

The Origins of Dinosaurs

At first earth was rather hostile to life. Then, about 3,000 million years ago, microscopic organisms developed in the oceans. Simple life forms came to inhabit the sea. Gradually, these life forms evolved into creatures that could move on land and creatures that could fly.

Terrible Lizard

The name dinosaur means "terrible lizard" and it's thought that dinosaurs evolved from reptiles. Reptiles survived during the Mesozoic era because they fully adapted themselves to the changing environment. The first reptiles appeared around 300 million years ago. They evolved from amphibians. Unlike amphibians, which had to spend some time in water for laying their eggs, reptiles developed hard scaly skin that helped them live on land. Moreover, they laid hard-shelled eggs that hatched on land. Petrolacosaurus, Milleretta are Scutosaurus are among the earliest reptiles.

Ancestors of Dinosaurs

Scientists say that the now extinct Thecodonts, or Archosaurs, that lived about 230 million years ago, are ancestors of crocodilians, pterosaurs and dinosaurs as well. They were meat-eating quadrupeds with long jaws and a long tail. These creatures were socket-toothed, which means that their teeth were set in sockets in the jawbones. This made the teeth less likely to be torn loose during feeding. Thecodonts also had scaly skin. They closely resembled the crocodile, but they actually evolved into dinosaurs.

The Acanthostega was one of the first vertebrates to have recognizable limbs and be capable of coming on land

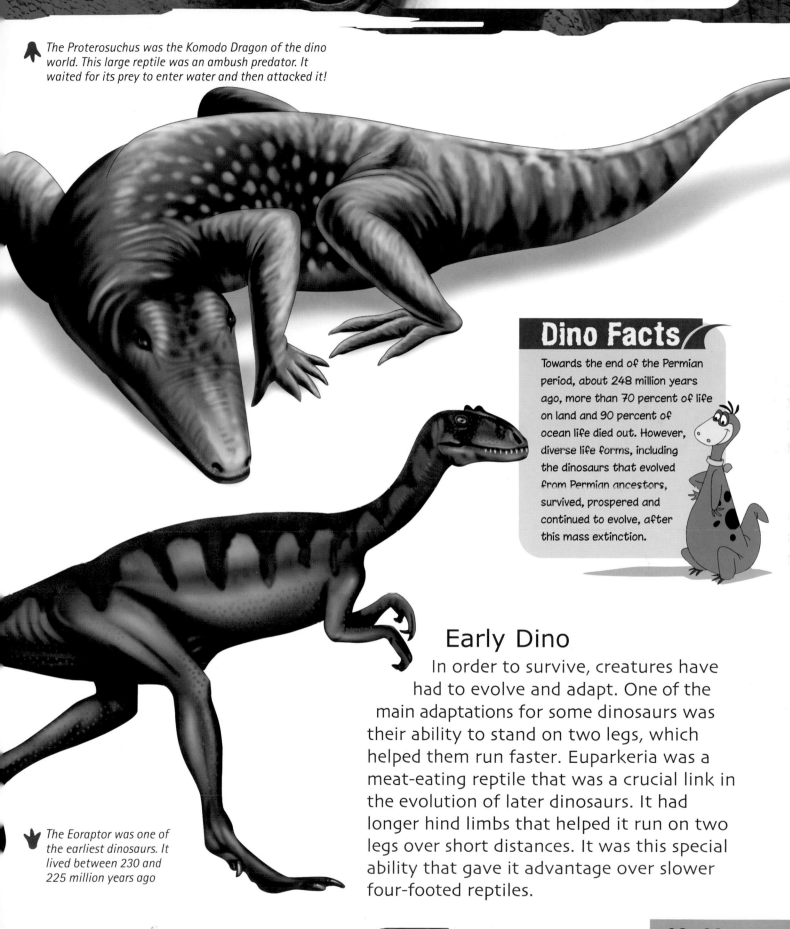

The Proterosuchus was the Komodo Dragon of the dino world. This large reptile was an ambush predator. It waited for its prey to enter water and then attacked it!

Dino Facts

Towards the end of the Permian period, about 248 million years ago, more than 70 percent of life on land and 90 percent of ocean life died out. However, diverse life forms, including the dinosaurs that evolved from Permian ancestors, survived, prospered and continued to evolve, after this mass extinction.

Early Dino

In order to survive, creatures have had to evolve and adapt. One of the main adaptations for some dinosaurs was their ability to stand on two legs, which helped them run faster. Euparkeria was a meat-eating reptile that was a crucial link in the evolution of later dinosaurs. It had longer hind limbs that helped it run on two legs over short distances. It was this special ability that gave it advantage over slower four-footed reptiles.

The Eoraptor was one of the earliest dinosaurs. It lived between 230 and 225 million years ago

Two of a Kind

Dinosaurs are classified according to the structure of their bones. There are two types of dinos — bird-hipped and reptile-hipped. Interestingly, it was the reptile-hipped dino that evolved into the birds we know today.

Bone Factor

Bird-hipped dinos are known as Ornithischians, and reptile-hipped dinos are called Saurischians. In Ornithischians, the pubis bone points downwards towards the tail, running parallel with the ischium. This feature is believed to have made the Ornithischians more stable while moving. In Saurischians, the pubis bone points downwards to the front.

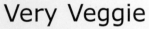

Pubis

Ischium

Diagram of an Ornithischian hip, showing the pubis bone and ischium running parallel

Very Veggie

All Ornithischian dinosaurs were herbivores. They evolved in the Triassic period and died out with the other dinos at the end of the Cretaceous period. Many of them walked on four legs (quadrupedal). Stegosaurus and Triceratops are well-known bird-hipped dinos. Dryosaurus and Pachycephalosaurus are examples of Ornithischians that moved on two legs.

The Triceratops had three horn – one short horn projected above its parrot-like beak and two longer horns above its eyes

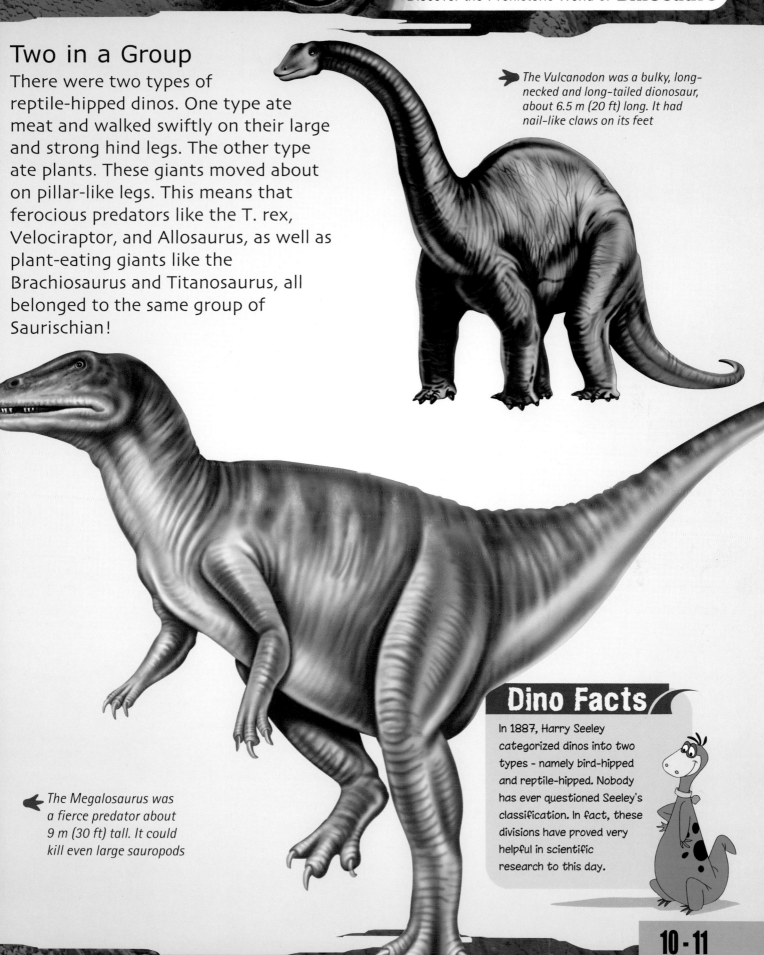

Two in a Group

There were two types of reptile-hipped dinos. One type ate meat and walked swiftly on their large and strong hind legs. The other type ate plants. These giants moved about on pillar-like legs. This means that ferocious predators like the T. rex, Velociraptor, and Allosaurus, as well as plant-eating giants like the Brachiosaurus and Titanosaurus, all belonged to the same group of Saurischian!

The Vulcanodon was a bulky, long-necked and long-tailed dionosaur, about 6.5 m (20 ft) long. It had nail-like claws on its feet

The Megalosaurus was a fierce predator about 9 m (30 ft) tall. It could kill even large sauropods

Dino Facts

In 1887, Harry Seeley categorized dinos into two types - namely bird-hipped and reptile-hipped. Nobody has ever questioned Seeley's classification. In fact, these divisions have proved very helpful in scientific research to this day.

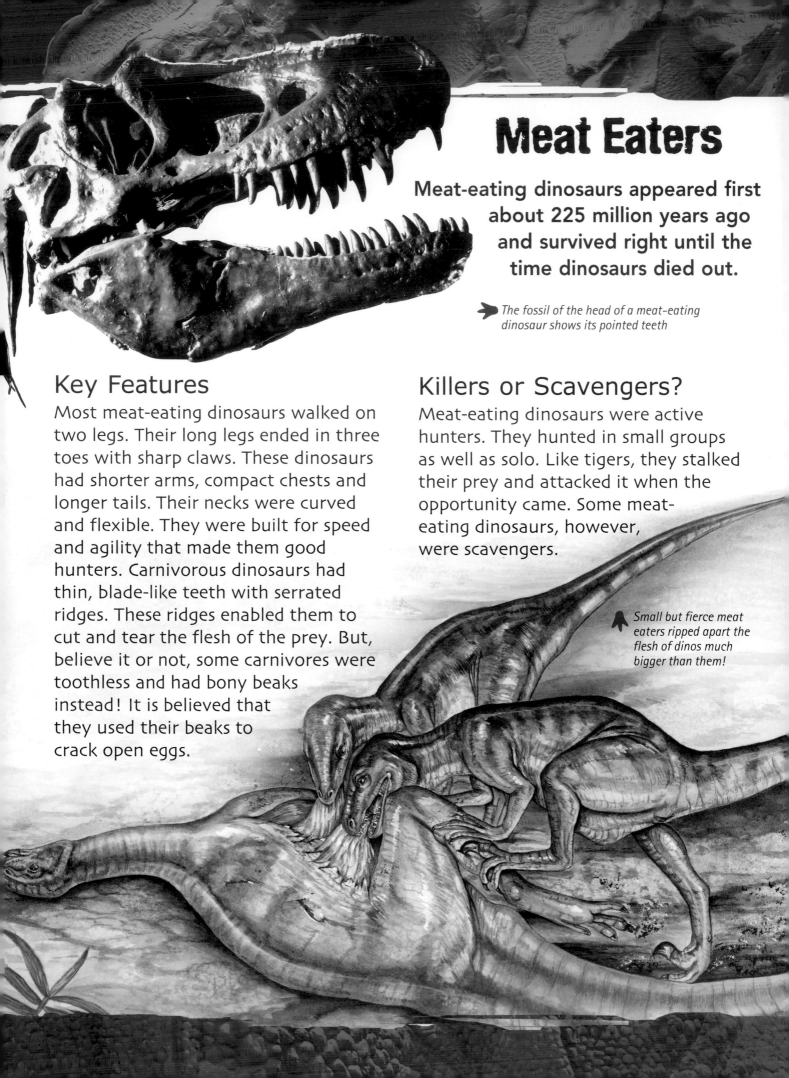

Meat Eaters

Meat-eating dinosaurs appeared first about 225 million years ago and survived right until the time dinosaurs died out.

➤ *The fossil of the head of a meat-eating dinosaur shows its pointed teeth*

Key Features

Most meat-eating dinosaurs walked on two legs. Their long legs ended in three toes with sharp claws. These dinosaurs had shorter arms, compact chests and longer tails. Their necks were curved and flexible. They were built for speed and agility that made them good hunters. Carnivorous dinosaurs had thin, blade-like teeth with serrated ridges. These ridges enabled them to cut and tear the flesh of the prey. But, believe it or not, some carnivores were toothless and had bony beaks instead! It is believed that they used their beaks to crack open eggs.

Killers or Scavengers?

Meat-eating dinosaurs were active hunters. They hunted in small groups as well as solo. Like tigers, they stalked their prey and attacked it when the opportunity came. Some meat-eating dinosaurs, however, were scavengers.

▲ *Small but fierce meat eaters ripped apart the flesh of dinos much bigger than them!*

Small and Big

The first meat-eating dinosaurs were quite small — barely 3 feet long! Eoraptor, Coelophysis and Herrerasaurus were some of the small meat-eating dinosaurs of the early Triassic period. Dinosaurs gradually grew in size. Their limbs became more slender, their brains became larger and their eyesight became stronger. Larger meat-eating dinosaurs began to appear in the Jurassic period. Dinosaurs such as Dilophosaurus, Gigantosaurus, Megalosaurus and Ceratosaurus were large meat-eating creatures. At 12 m (40 ft) long, Allosaurus was the largest meat-eating dinosaur of the Cretaceous period.

Dino Facts

Meat-eating dinosaurs are collectively known as 'theropods' - meaning beast-footed. The famous American fossil hunter, Othniel Charles Marsh, is attributed with first making this classification in 1881.

◄ *The Allosaurus had razor-sharp claws, about 15 cm (6 in) long, and razor-sharp teeth, about 10 cm (4 in) long*

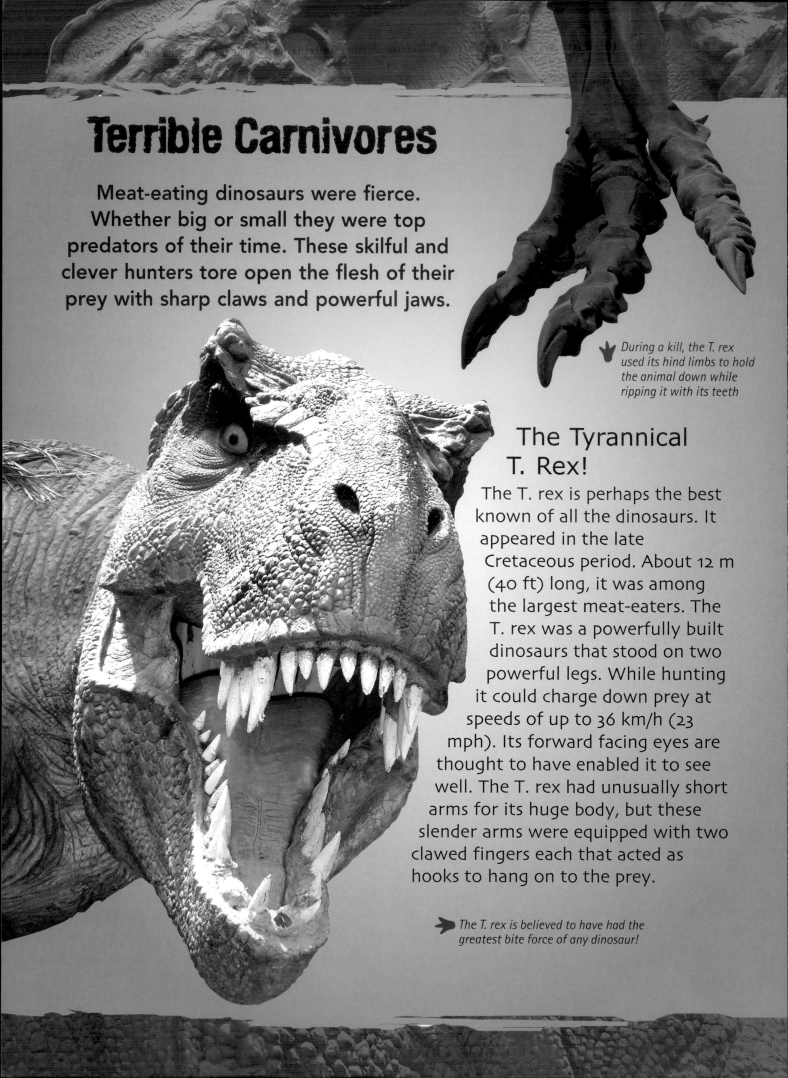

Terrible Carnivores

Meat-eating dinosaurs were fierce. Whether big or small they were top predators of their time. These skilful and clever hunters tore open the flesh of their prey with sharp claws and powerful jaws.

During a kill, the T. rex used its hind limbs to hold the animal down while ripping it with its teeth

The Tyrannical T. Rex!

The T. rex is perhaps the best known of all the dinosaurs. It appeared in the late Cretaceous period. About 12 m (40 ft) long, it was among the largest meat-eaters. The T. rex was a powerfully built dinosaurs that stood on two powerful legs. While hunting it could charge down prey at speeds of up to 36 km/h (23 mph). Its forward facing eyes are thought to have enabled it to see well. The T. rex had unusually short arms for its huge body, but these slender arms were equipped with two clawed fingers each that acted as hooks to hang on to the prey.

The T. rex is believed to have had the greatest bite force of any dinosaur!

Dino Size

The Deinonychus was barely 2 m (6.6 ft) in length but was a formidable predator nonetheless. It moved swiftly on two hind legs. Its most distinctive feature was the curved claw on the second toe of each foot. The claw was about 13 cm (5 in) long. During a hunt the Deinonychus would slash its prey with these claws. In fact the name Deinonychus means 'terrible claw'. These clever creatures hunted in packs and were able to wound an animal many times their own size.

Dino Facts

Did you know that one carnivorous dinosaur preferred fish to meat? This was the Baronyx. About 10 m (33 ft) in length, this dinosaur had killer claws about 35 cm (14 in) long! It also had a narrow head and a snout like a crocodile. The spoon-shaped tip of its mouth helped it to scoop up fish from the water.

➤ The Deinonychus had a rather large brain: scientists believe that it was one of the smartest dinos

Other Carnivores

Many species of dinosaurs were part of the group that included all the meat-eaters. Dromaeosaurs, commonly known as raptors, and Orthinomimids, were two such species.

What's in a Name?

The name Dromaeosaur means 'running lizard'. Most of them were around 2 m (6.5 feet) long. These creatures were among the fiercest of all dinosaurs. The long, deadly claws on their feet and their big hands came in handy when they hunted in the jungle. Because they were small, most raptors hunted in packs. They were shrewd hunters. While on a hunt, they would look for the weakest prey.

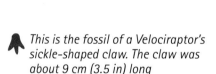

This is the fossil of a Velociraptor's sickle-shaped claw. The claw was about 9 cm (3.5 in) long

Many Kinds

Fossils have confirmed that there were many raptors in the Cretaceous period. The Velociraptor, Pyroraptor and Utahraptor are just a few of the Dromaeosaurs of the period. The Velociraptor was a fierce predator armed with sharp serrated teeth and a large sickle-shaped claw on the second toe of each foot. It used this claw to slash at its prey, wounding it until it gave up running away.

Velociraptor means 'speedy feet'. It was a fast running bipedal dinosaur. This small dino was about 2 m (6 ft) long and 1 m (3 ft) tall

The toothless Orthinomimids used their bony beaks to nibble on a diet of insects, small reptiles and mammals, as well as fruit, eggs, seeds and leaves

Birds or Not?

The Orthinomimids or 'bird mimics' looked similar to some of the flightless birds of today, such as the ostrich and emu. They had long legs, slender arms and toothless beaks. Their long, stiff tails enabled them to maintain balance when they ran. The Ornithomimus, Gallimimus, Deinocheirus and Struthiomimus are some well-known Orthinomimids of the Cretaceous period. Because these dinosaurs were toothless, they could not rely wholly on meat for survival.

Dino Facts

The Oviraptor was a bird-like dinosaur. It was probably covered with fluffy down and may have had feathers on some parts of its body. It also had a bony crest. Its arms may have been wing-like. It got its name, which means 'egg stealer', from a misconception that it stole Protoceratops's eggs. But, in truth, the Oviraptor was a doting parent.

Plant Eaters

Plant-eating dinosaurs appeared about 220 million years ago. They were much larger than the biggest meat-eaters. These giants thrived during the Jurassic period, which saw the growth of a variety of plants.

Pillars of Strength

Othniel Charles Marsh included these plant-eaters in a group named sauropods, or 'lizard feet'. Unlike its meat-eating relatives, this herbivore walked on all fours. It had thick, pillar-like legs, a long neck and a long tail. But it had a relatively small head.

The plant-eating dinosaurs were much more numerous and more diverse than the meat-eating ones

Food for All

These herbivores fed on ferns, mosses and leaves of tall trees. They used their teeth to pluck leaves from branches. The biggest ones, with long, flexible necks, could graze on the leaves of the tallest trees. The smaller ones fed on smaller plants and trees. These dinosaurs didn't need to compete for food as there was always plenty of food for all.

Fight Me if You Can!

Because these dinosaurs were heavy, they could not outrun their meat-eating relatives. But if they lacked speed, they had enormous strength. When attacked they lashed out with great power at their enemy. They used their tail as a whip or feet as giant crushers to inflict serious injuries on their attacker. Meat-eating dinosaurs usually stayed away from them.

Without plants there would have been no dinos. The herbivores ate plants and the carnivores fed on the smaller vegetarian dinos

Dino Facts

The teeth of some plant-eating dinosaurs were not designed for chewing leaves, so they swallowed their food straight down. Many of them swallowed stones as well to aid digestion. These stones helped to crush the leaves in their stomach into a soft pulp.

Brachiosaurus

The Brachiosaurus is among the most well known dinosaurs. It was the giraffe of the dinosaur world, using its long and flexible neck to pluck leaves from treetops.

See how small an adult man would look compared to the Brachiosaurus!

Creature Features

The Brachiosaurus was a huge dinosaur, about 25 m (82 ft) long and 16 m (50 ft) tall. It weighed about 16.5 tons. This creature's long neck swayed gracefully. It had a bulky body and four pillar-like legs, but a relatively small head. Unlike most other sauropods, its front legs were longer than its hind legs. So its body sloped down towards its tail. Interestingly, its name, which means, 'arm lizard', originated from its longer fore limbs.

Veggie Meal

Brachiosaurus usually moved around in large herds. They spent most of their time searching for food. These dinosaurs ate ginkgo tree leaves, conifer needles, palm fronds and low-growing vegetation. The incredibly long neck of this creature helped it graze on leaves that grew high up and also cover a large area of foliage without even having to move its feet. It had 52 chisel-like teeth with which it tugged and nipped at leaves. It swallowed its food whole, without chewing it.

It is believed that herds of Brachiosaurus migrated to regions with more food when they depleted their local food supply

Dino Facts

The Brachiosaurus had nostrils on top of it head! This must have given it quite a keen sense of smell. The Brachiosaurus could probably smell food and other animals even before seeing them!

Huge Herbivores

There were many species of plant-eating dinosaurs. These dinosaurs evolved during the Jurassic and Cretaceous periods.

One of the Longest

At about 27 m (89 ft) long the Diplodocus was one of the longest dinosaurs. Like most plant-eaters, it had a long neck. The Diplodocus' tail was about 14 m (46 ft) long - equal to about half the creature's length! When these dinosaurs moved, their neck and tail were more or less at the same level and they must have looked like walking suspension bridges! The name Diplodocus, which means 'double beam', owes its origin to this dinosaur's long and flexible tail that had an extra length of bone beneath the tailbones. When attacked, this creature lashed its tail to scare the attacker away.

High or Low?

Until recently many scientists believed that the Diplodocus, like the Brachiosaurus, raised its long neck to pluck leaves from the tops of tall trees. But recent studies of its fossils suggest that the Diplodocus could not raise its neck much above shoulder height. This means that, unlike most other plant eaters, this creature was incapable of reaching leaves on treetops. So the Diplodocus must have lived on a diet of ferns and low-growing plants. This meant that it did not have to compete with the Brachiosaurus for food, which is probably how both giants managed to survive.

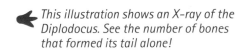

This illustration shows an X-ray of the Diplodocus. See the number of bones that formed its tail alone!

➤ *The Diplodocus was actually of a lighter build than other dinos its size: it weighed between 10 and 20 tons*

Dino Facts

Bones of the Titanosaurus were first discovered near the town of Jabalpur in India in 1871. They could not be matched with the bones of other dinosaurs found up until that point, so scientists concluded that they must belong to a new dinosaur. The new dinosaur was named Titanosaurus Indicus, or the 'giant lizard from India', in 1877 by Richard Lydekker.

Tapering Tail

The Titanosaurus appeared in the late Cretaceous period. It was about 20 m (66 ft) long. Like the Diplodocus, it had a whip-like, tapering tail. When attacked, it used its tail as a weapon, flicking it wildly to scare the attacker away. If that didn't work, then it used its giant, strong legs to kick the attacker. Titanosaurus belonged to the group of Titanosaurs or 'gigantic lizards'. Some Titanosaurs were 30 m (100 ft) long! Titanosaurs had bony armor on their body and their skin was studded with small armored plates for protection.

➤ *Titanosauruses get their name from the early Greek gods, called Titans*

Weapons and Armor

Over the ages dinosaurs developed many interesting features. In general, meat-eaters developed horns and talons to hunt, while plant-eaters developed armor to protect themselves from attack!

Armor-plated Dinosaurs

Nodosaurs were the first fully armored dinosaurs. They appeared about 175 million years ago. Their name means 'node lizards'. They get their name from the many lumpy nodules of bones embedded in their skin. The other group of armored dinosaurs were known as Ankylosaurs. The armor on Nodosaurs and Ankylosaurs comprised of flat or raised bony plates. The largest plates and spines were usually on the neck and smaller ones on the back and tail. Spaces between the plates were filled with bone pads so that the dinosaur would still be flexible enough to move.

◄ It is believed that the Stegosaur's upright plates helped it control body temperature through thermoregulation

The Euoplocephalus had a bony club at the tip of its tail to hit out with!

Scuted Dinosaurs

Plated dinosaurs include the Stegosaur family. These medium-to-large plant eaters had many upright bony plates, known as scutes, growing from their skin, on their backs and along their tails. These plates were arranged differently from Stegosaur to Stegosaur. Some had pairs of plates arranged along the spine to the tail, while others had plates running along the sides of their bodies. This armor was useful because it could be used for defense as well as attack. Scientists also believe that these plates were used in courtship displays.

Horned Dinosaurs

Also known as Ceratopsians, horned dinosaurs were widespread in the Cretaceous period. They ranged from the size of a turkey to the size of an elephant. While some dinosaurs of this group had horns on their heads, others had frills of bone around their necks – but all of them had a skull with a beak-like snout. Scientists believe that apart from helping in self-defense, the horns and frills were used to attract mates. During courtship battles the horned dinosaurs would lock their horns and push hard to decide the strongest.

The Triceratops would charge at predators much bigger than itself in self protection!

Dino Facts

The Scelidosaurus is thought to be an ancestor of the Stegosaurs. Its body was studded with many small body plates. Some of these were ridged, others cone shaped. Unlike the plates of the Stegosaurs, the plates of the Scelidosaurus were not pointed.

Adapted to the Environment

There were many species of plated, armored and horned dinosaurs. Each of them was uniquely adapted to its environment.

Stegosaurus

The Stegosaurus was the largest dinosaur of the plated Stegosaur family. About 9 m (30 ft) in length, this slow-moving herbivore was a long, low animal with a small head. Its hind legs were twice as long as its fore legs. It had 17 plates of varying sizes stretching all the way from its neck to the tail. No one knows for sure how the plates were arranged. They may have been in one straight row, in a staggered row or in two rows. This dinosaur also had two pairs of horn-covered spines at the end of its thick, stiff tail. When in danger of being attacked, the Stegosaurus probably flicked its tail in defense.

With plates and spikes on the body, horns on the head and club-like tail, the Ankylosaurus was fully protected from its predators!

Ankylosaurus

The Ankylosaurus was about 10 m (33 ft) long. It was one of the largest armored dinosaurs. This dinosaur was a squat animal with a wide, barrel-shaped body. It had a wide skull and a short neck. Its fore legs were shorter than its hind legs. The height of this dinosaur allowed it to feed only on plants that were low to the ground. The whole of its topside was heavily covered with thick, oval plates embedded in its leathery skin. Only its underbelly was unplated.

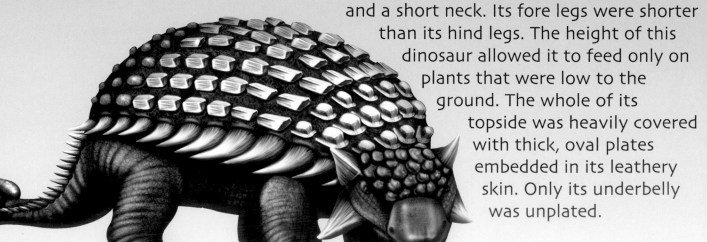

Triceratops

The name Triceratops means 'three horned face'. Triceratops is the best-known horned dinosaur. This plant-eater was about 9 m (30 ft) long, and had a bulky body. It weighed about 9 tons. This dinosaur had a parrot-like beak, many chewing teeth and strong jaws. It used its small teeth to chew plants before swallowing them. It had a short tail and stout legs with hooved feet. This creature had a neck frill with bony bumps. It also had three horns. The two above its eyes were about 1 m (3 ft) long. But its nose horn was much shorter. When threatened, this dinosaur probably charged at its enemy with its horns.

The Stegosaurus had a toothless beak to nip at plants and small cheek-teeth to chew them

Dino Facts

It is believed that the plates of the Stegosaurus were covered with skin through which blood vessels ran. So, when this creature was threatened, extra blood was pumped through the vessels. This extra blood may have caused the plates to turn pink, sending out signals to other animals.

With its set of horns, the Triceratops resembled the rhinoceros

Bone-Headed Dinos

Over the years, a new type of dinosaur evolved. These dinosaurs were known as Pachycephalosaurs or 'thick-headed dinosaurs'. They got their name from their extremely thick skulls. They used their skulls to defend themselves from their enemies.

Head Bangers

The Stegoceras was about 2m (6.6 ft) long. It was a bone-headed dinosaur. A young Stegoceras had a relatively flat skull but as it grew, its bony dome became more and more prominent. The thickest part of the skull was 6cm (2.5 in) thick. This dinosaur had a strange bony ridge at the back of its skull. Male bone-headed dinosaurs head-butted one another when they fought for territories or mates. At times they even head-butted for fun!

Dino Facts

Stygimoloch was the only Pachycephalosaur with spikes on its head, which measured from 10-15 cm (4-6 in) long. Its head also had many bumpy nodules.

See the Stegoceras ramming their thick skulls into each other to decide the strongest one in the group

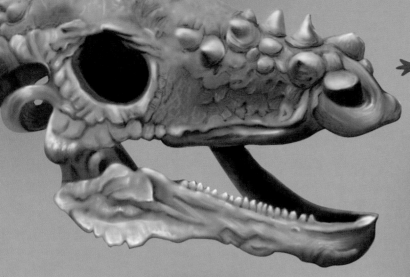

> *The Pachycephalosaurus was about 4.6 m (15 ft) long and weighed about 430 kg (950 lbs). It had distinctive bumpy knobs on its snout and along the rear of its skull*

Easy to Grasp

The Stegoceras moved about on two long legs. Its shorter arms had five fingers that helped it in grasping plants and pulling them towards its mouth. The claws on its fingers were used to dig up roots and other underground vegetation.

Biggest of Them all

The Pachycephalosaurus, a species of Pachycephalosaur, was one of the last bone-headed dinosaurs. The fossil of its skull proves that it had the largest skull of all bone-heads. Its skull was quite long — about 60 cm (2 ft)! And the bone that formed the dome was 25 cm (10 in) thick!

Of Teeth and Bill

During the Jurassic and Cretaceous periods a new category of dinosaurs evolved. These dinos, called Ornithopods, were the first plant-eaters to have true chewing teeth. They also had cheek pouches that helped them chew foodbetter.

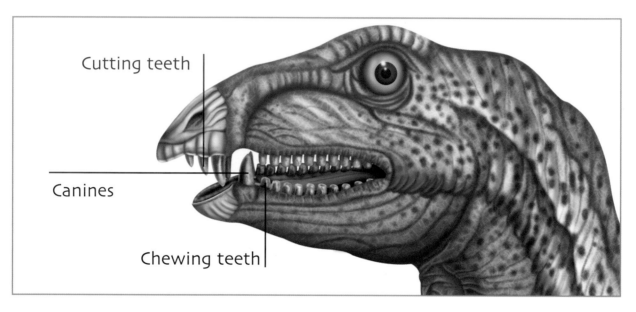

Cutting teeth

Canines

Chewing teeth

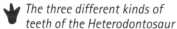 *The three different kinds of teeth of the Heterodontosaur*

Talk of Teeth

Ornithopods are divided into four different groups: the Heterodontosaur, the Hypsilophodont, the Iguanodont and the Hadrosaur. Heterodontosaurs had three kinds of teeth: cutting teeth, which were chisel-shaped; chewing teeth, which were ridged; and tusk-like canines. Only male Heterodontosaurs had tusks, which they probably used to spear prey and in courtship displays.

Teeth to Grind

Hypsilophodonts did not have any teeth at the front of their mouths so they bit off plants using their bony beaks. For chewing, they had ridged, chisel-shaped teeth. They chewed like today's cows and giraffes. Their jaws came together, with the upper jaw sliding outwards, moving in a circular motion. This helped to grind the food quickly and reduce it to a juicy pulp. Like Hypsilophodonts, Iguanodonts bit off plants with their bony beaks. Their small, molar-like teeth helped grind them into a pulp.

Dino Facts

The Maiasaura, the best-known Hadrosaur, was a caring parent. It made nests by scooping up soil. This dinosaur packed vegetation to provide a cushion for its eggs. It also covered its eggs with vegetation. When the plants rotted, they produced heat. This heat helped to incubate the eggs.

Duck-billed Dinos

Hadrosaurs had duck-like beaks which were broad and flat. These creatures also had about 1,600 teeth packed tightly into their jaws! Their teeth were arranged in groups of three across the jaw. This arrangement helped them crush and grind their food easily. They also had new teeth lined up below the jaw to replace the old ones that fell out.

➤ The Iguanodon had a conical thumb spike on each hand about 5 to 15 cm (2-6 in) long. This may have been used for defense or in obtaining food

Look I Can Fly!

Dinosaurs could not fly. But there were other reptiles during the age of dinos that could fly. These reptiles were Pterosaurs. The front limbs or 'arms' of Pterosaurs evolved into wings that helped them fly.

The Pterosaurs had hollow bones that made them light. They are also believed to have had large brains and good eyesight

Flying Limbs

A Pterosaur's wing consisted of tough but stretchy skin. This skin was attached along each side of the body from the shoulder to the leg. This looked quite similar to a modern bat's wing. The wing was stretched out by the bones of the long arm, the wrist and the hugely extended fourth finger. Pterosaurs were carnivores. Their diet mainly consisted of fish. They also fed on crabs, molluscs and plankton. On land they scavenged on dead animals. Early Pterosaurs appeared in the Triassic period but died out at the end of the Jurassic period. After this, several species of more advanced Pterosaurs appeared in the late Jurassic period and died out with the dinosaurs.

Dino Facts

Quetzalcoatlus was the largest Pterosaur. It had a wingspan of 11-15 m (36-49 ft)! To compare, the largest wingspan seen today belongs to the albatross at about 3 m (10 ft).

Elongated
fourth finger

Bony crest on
head. May have
acted as rudder
while flying

Birds or Not?

Though Pterosaurs could fly like birds,
they were very different from birds. Their
wings were supported mainly by finger
bones rather than arm bones like those of
birds. A Pterosaur's body was covered by a
kind of fur that kept it warm. These
reptiles did not have feathers. Even their
tails had bones and lacked feathers.

Wing made of
leathery membrane

Small tail

Legs for walking on land

Fingers with claws
to grip

*Despite its huge size,
the Quetzalcoatlus'
skeleton was lightly
built. This made it a
very good soarer,
capable of covering
large distances*

Different Moves

Some Pterosaurs had long and slender wings that
helped them soar and glide easily. Like the albatross,
these reptiles used thermals, or updrafts of warm air,
to fly effortlessly. Other Pterosaurs had short and
wide wings with powerful flapping muscles to help
them fly. All Pterosaurs had large chest muscles that
helped them flap their wings when they flew.

Why Did Dinos Disappear?

What is for certain is that dinosaurs became extinct. Exactly how they died out is hotly debated by experts to this day. The giants that once ruled the earth now exist only as fossils. Scientists have come up with several theories about their extinction.

The Rock From Space

According to the popular asteroid theory, an asteroid slammed into earth from space. This impact sent huge clouds of dust and debris into the air. The skies darkened and prevented sunlight from reaching earth. This caused plants to die, which led to the death of the herbivores. The meat-eaters soon died out too.

In theory, a large enough asteriod striking the earth would have been capable of wiping out the dinosaurs

Dino Facts

The change in vegetation is also believed to be an important cause of the death of dinosaurs. Flowering plants appeared during the Cretaceous period. This displaced most conifers and many other plants. Some herbivorous dinosaurs, like the Edmontosaurus, ate only conifers and they starved.

Deadly Rays and Flaming Earth

Another extinction theory involves deadly radiation from space that bathed the earth. When a huge star reaches the end of it life it becomes a fireball called a supernova. At this stage it sends out dangerous radiations at very high speed. A supernova explosion may have occurred 65 million years ago, which may have killed all the dinosaurs on earth. Yet another theory relates the widespread, long-lasting volcanic eruptions as the cause of extinction.

Volcanic eruptions emit poisonous choking fumes, which may have killed the dinos

A dinosaur fossil embedded in soil

Other Theories

Some scientists believe that dinosaurs were struck down by a new and deadly disease that they were unable to fight, ultimately causing their extinction. Some are of the opinion that rapid climatic change caused by the drifting continents froze the dinosaurs to death. Yet others believe that increasing numbers of small mammals ate the eggs of dinosaurs causing them to disappear.

From Bone to Stone

Fossils are the preserved remains of animals, plants or other organisms. Dinosaur fossils have been preserved over millions of years. Even today, new discoveries are being made, constantly adding to our understanding of dinos.

Dino Facts

Would you believe that the skin, muscles, tendons and organs of dinosaurs have also been preserved as fossils? It is rare to find such fossils as soft tissue usually decomposes before fossilisation. Fossilized impressions of dinosaur skin are called dinosaur "mummies".

It is a rare and special find to discover the fossil of a complete dinosaur skeleton

Preserved in Stone

When a dinosaur died, it may have been quickly buried in mud or sand. Over many years, layers of more mud, sand and rock covered the remains. Due to the action of weather and minerals over a very long period of time, the bones decayed. The chemicals and minerals of the bones fused with the minerals of the sand and rock. This way the bones changed to hard stone, or fossils. Only the hardest parts of the dinosaur, such as bones, teeth, claws and horns, became fossilized. Studying them we learn a lot about those dinos. The conditions for a dinosaur to become a fossil are quite rare, so any find is an exciting event.

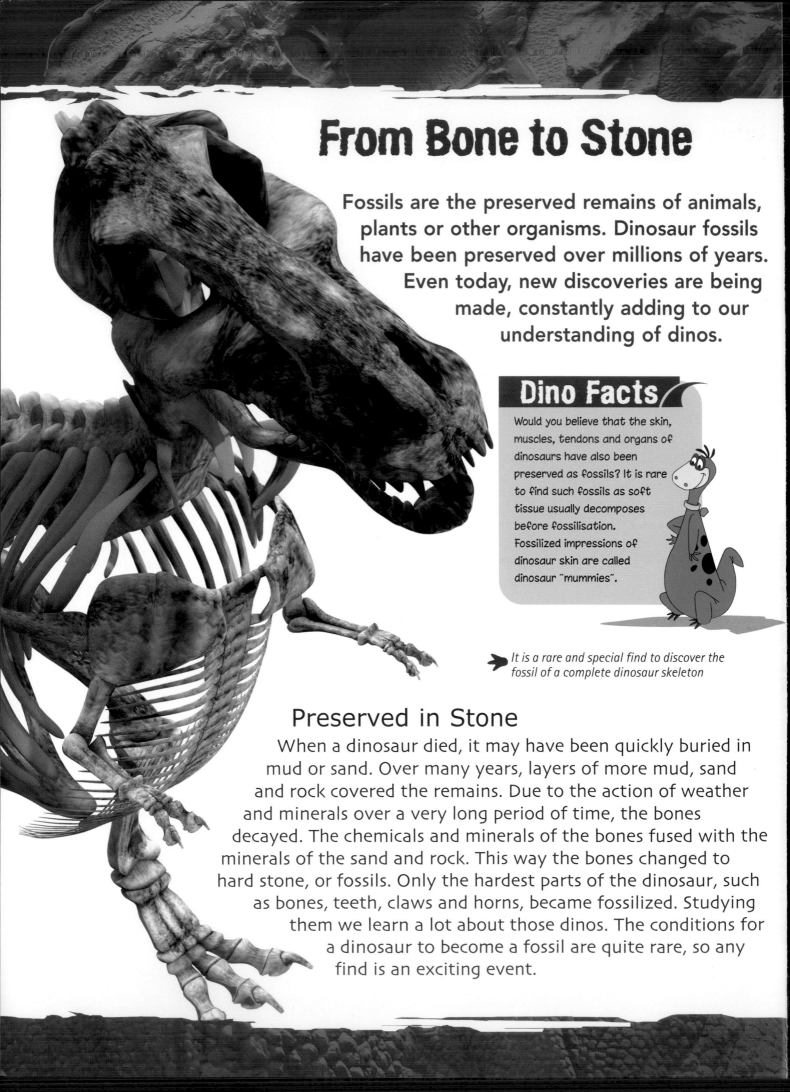

What Do Fossils Look Like?

A fossil has the same shape as the original object but it is actually a rock! So, a fossil is a rocky model of an ancient object. The color, texture and weight of a fossil varies greatly from the original object. The color and texture of the fossil depends on what minerals formed it. For example, the Kakuru dinosaur bone became fossilized in the beautiful opal stone!

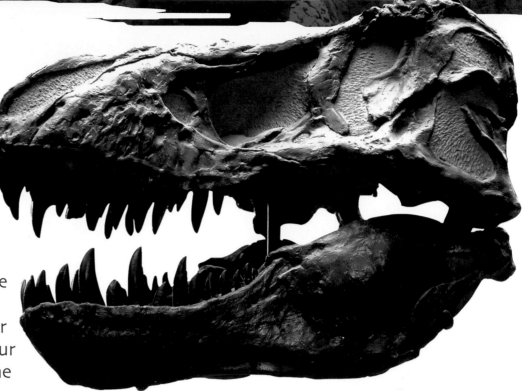

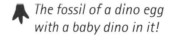 *Because fossils are rocks, they are heavier than the original object*

The fossil of a dino egg with a baby dino in it!

Types of Fossils

Fossils of dinosaurs generally fall into two categories — cast and mould fossils and trace fossils. In a mould fossil, a body part is buried by sediments that form a rock around it. When the body part decays, it leaves a hole or impression of the same shape. A cast fossil is formed when this depression is slowly filled with minerals leaving a stone of the shape of the body part. Trace fossils are records of the movement and behavior of dinosaurs, such as their footprints and claw marks. These help us learn about their speed, the number of toes they had, etc.

The image shows the footprints of a dinosaur that have become preserved in stone over millions of years

Fossil Hunters

People started finding dinosaur bones thousands of years ago. Indeed, more than 2,000 years ago in China, they were known as 'dragon bones'. It was as late as 1800 that fossil collecting became well known in Europe.

Scientific Study

In 1822, Gideon Mantell, a doctor and keen fossil hunter from England, found teeth and bones that he thought belonged to a huge lizard. In 1825 he named this creature 'Iguanodon'. William Buckland, a rock and fossil expert, found the jawbone and teeth of another huge lizard that he classified as 'Megalosaurus'. In 1841, Richard Owen realised that these creatures were not lizards at all but a separate group of reptiles that he named Dinosaurs!

An expert carefully and delicately brushes away the soil from a fossilized dinosaur claw

All Across the World

By the 1860s fossil diggers in North America were excavating rare dinosaur fossils. Charles Marsh and Edward Drinker Cope gave dinosaur fossil hunting a big boost by discovering the fossils of 130 kinds of dinosaurs, mainly in the rocky "Badlands" of the US Midwest. By 1900, many fossil diggers were digging in Africa. In the 1920s, quite a few excavations were carried out in China. South America and Australia also joined the hunt for dinosaur fossils. Since 1991 dinosaur fossils have also been found in the Antarctic.

"Badlands", in the US, where many dino fossils have been found

Excavating Treasure

Excavation is a long, tiring process. A newly found fossil has to be carefully freed from the rest of the rocky debris. Fossil experts use picks, shovels, hammers and even explosives to get rid of the overlying rock. When a fossil is discovered, small hand tools, such as awls and trowels, are used with utmost care so as not to damage the fossil.

A lab where experts do a final cleaning and test of the fossils. Plaster is often used to complete damaged parts

Dino Facts

William Parker Foulke was the first to put together the first near-complete dinosaur skeleton. Using bones found by some work men in Haddonfield in 1838, and combining them with the bones he discovered in 1858, Foulke built this amazing skeleton. Professor Joseph Leidy named it Hadrosaurus fouki.

Dinos Around Us

Dinosaurs are long-since extinct but they continue to fascinate us. Fossils and models of these giant creatures are kept at museums, and there is no shortage of dinosaur representations in popular culture.

A wonderful collection of dinosaur fossils and models in a museum

In the Museum

Dinosaur fossils are mainly used for scientific research. But they also enjoy a prominent place in museums and exhibitions. Spectacular life-size models entertain and inform adults and children alike. While the skeleton of the dinosaur is put together on the basis of fossils, the skin and outer appearance is calculated by experts based on scientific evidence. Modern technology even helps to make some models move and roar!

Dino Facts

Making a model of a dinosaur is quite a difficult job. For this one needs to know many things, like whether the dinosaur normally stood upright or crouched down, if it could bend its tail and so on. Putting together a dinosaur skeleton calls for special mounting skills. An armature, or plastic or metallic frame, is used for this purpose.

Dinos Everywhere

Dinosaur storybooks, toys, board games and video games are extremely popular with children and adults alike. Moviemakers have been presenting dinosaurs in movies for years. Some of these explore the life and habitat of these giant creatures, while others show what it would be like to have them around today. This has become possible with the aid of computer generated technology.

Dino Facts

The North American Museum of Ancient Life, in Utah, is supposed to be the largest dinosaur museum in the world. It has more than 60 mounted dinosaur skeletons and thousands of ancient fossils. The museum also showcases the various prehistoric eras and offers hands-on learning activities. The museum also has a movie screen and theater, featuring a variety of 3-D movies and other specialty films.

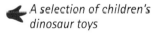
← *A selection of children's dinosaur toys*

Spread Across the World

Though most dinosaur fossils have been found in North America, fossilized dinosaurs have been found on all the continents.

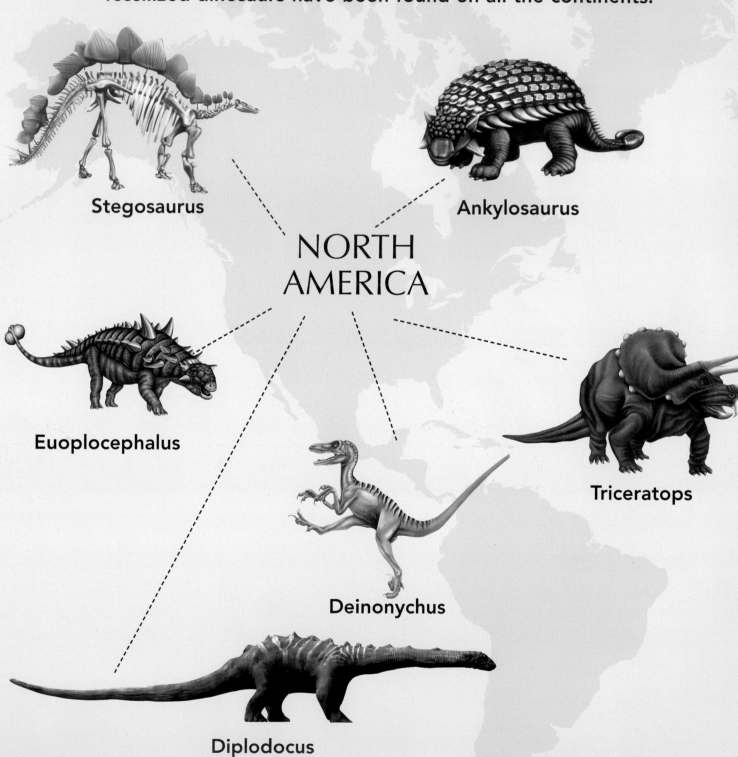

Stegosaurus

Ankylosaurus

NORTH AMERICA

Euoplocephalus

Triceratops

Deinonychus

Diplodocus

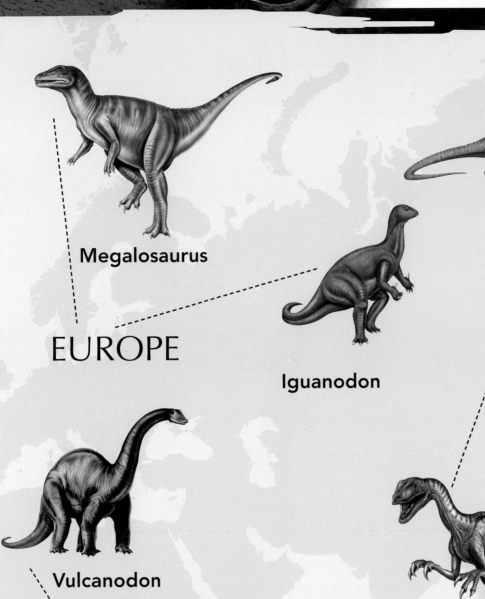

Megalosaurus

EUROPE

Iguanodon

Titanosaurus

ASIA

Vulcanodon

Velociraptor

AFRICA

Spinosaurus

Brachiosaurus

Glossary

Amphibians: Creatures that spend part of their lives in water and part on land

Ancestor: One from whom a creature is descended

Asteroid: Rock from space

Bipedal: Creatures that walk on two legs

Bulky: Heavy

Carnivores: Animals that feed on other animals

Continental drift: The gradual movement of the earth's continents

Decay: Waste away

Distinctive: Unique

Enormous: Huge

Equipped: To be fitted with

Extinct: To die out

Fierce: Scary

Flexible: Capable of being bended

Herbivores: Animals that feed on plants

Lash out: To strike

Mammals: Warm blooded animals, the females of which produce milk to feed the young

Mortally wounded: Injury that leads to death

Predator: Animals that hunt and kill other animals for food

Prey: Animals that are hunted

Quadruped: Animals that walk on four feet

Reptiles: Cold blooded animals

Savage: Cruel

Scavengers: Animals that feed on dead animals

Skeleton: Body structure made up of bones of various shapes and sizes

Slender: Thin

Vertebrates: Animals that have bones

Index